HAL•LEONARD

JAZZ PLAY-ALONG®

Book & Audio for B♭, E♭, C and Bass Clef Instruments

VOLUME 6

PLAYBACK+

Speed • Pitch • Balance • Loop

Jazz Classics
With Easy Changes

10 Jazz Classics

Arranged and Produced by
Mark Taylor

To access audio, visit:
www.halleonard.com/mylibrary

3041-9523-0684-9472

T0033992

ISBN 978-0-634-04405-2

HAL•LEONARD®

Visit Hal Leonard Online at
www.halleonard.com

World headquarters, contact:
Hal Leonard
7777 West Bluemound Road
Milwaukee, WI 53213
Email: info@halleonard.com

In Europe, contact:
Hal Leonard Europe Limited
1 Red Place
London, W1K 6PL
Email: info@halleonardeurope.com

In Australia, contact:
Hal Leonard Australia Pty. Ltd.
4 Lentara Court
Cheltenham, Victoria, 3192 Australia
Email: info@halleonard.com.au

JAZZ CLASSICS
WITH EASY CHANGES

Volume 6

Arranged and Produced by
Mark Taylor

Featured Players:

Graham Breedlove–Trumpet
John Delsame–Tenor Sax
Tony Nalker–Piano
Jim Roberts–Bass
Steve Fidyk–Drums

HOW TO USE THE AUDIO:

Each song has <u>two</u> tracks:

1) Split Track/Demonstration

Woodwind, Brass, Keyboard, and **Mallet Players** can use this track as a learning tool for melody style and inflection.

Bass Players can learn and perform with this track – remove the recorded bass track by turning down the volume on the LEFT channel.

Keyboard and **Guitar Players** can learn and perform with this track – remove the recorded piano part by turning down the volume on the RIGHT channel.

2) Backing Track

Soloists or **Groups** can learn and perform with this accompaniment track with the RHYTHM SECTION only.

BLUE TRAIN

C VERSION

BY JOHN COLTRANE

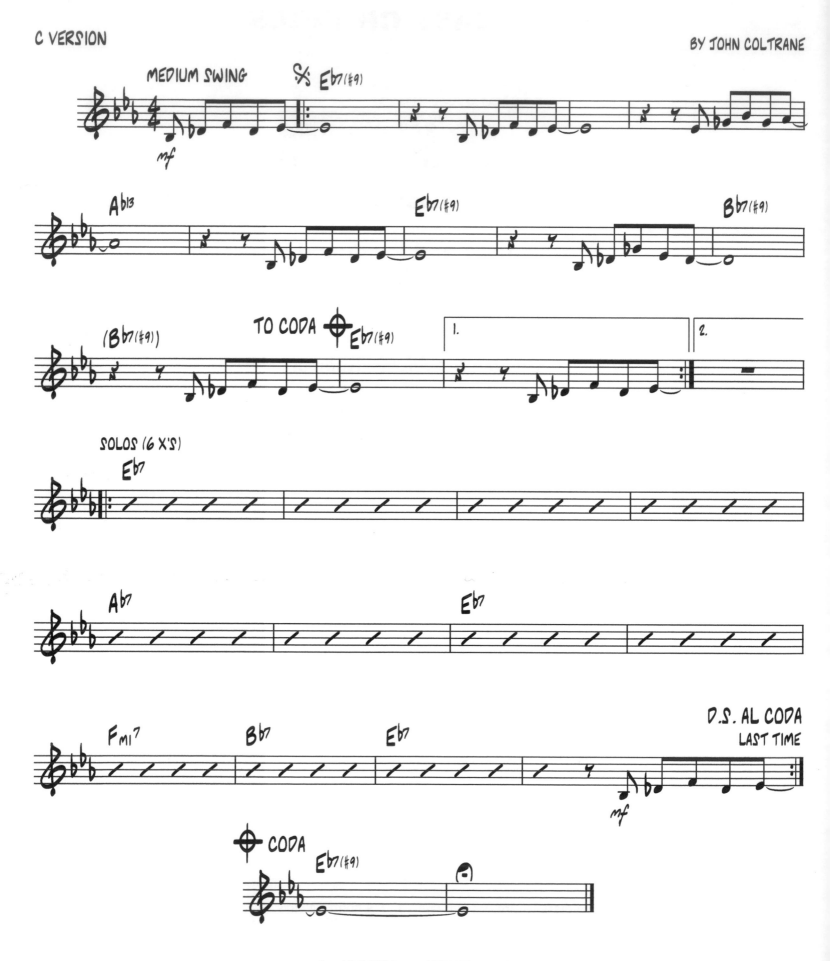

COMIN' HOME BABY

C VERSION

By Bob Dorough and Ben Tucker

FOOTPRINTS

C VERSION

BY WAYNE SHORTER

IMPRESSIONS

BY JOHN COLTRANE

C VERSION

Killer Joe

C VERSION

BY BENNY GOLSON

MOANIN'

C VERSION

BY BOBBY TIMMONS

SIDEWINDER

C VERSION

BY LEE MORGAN

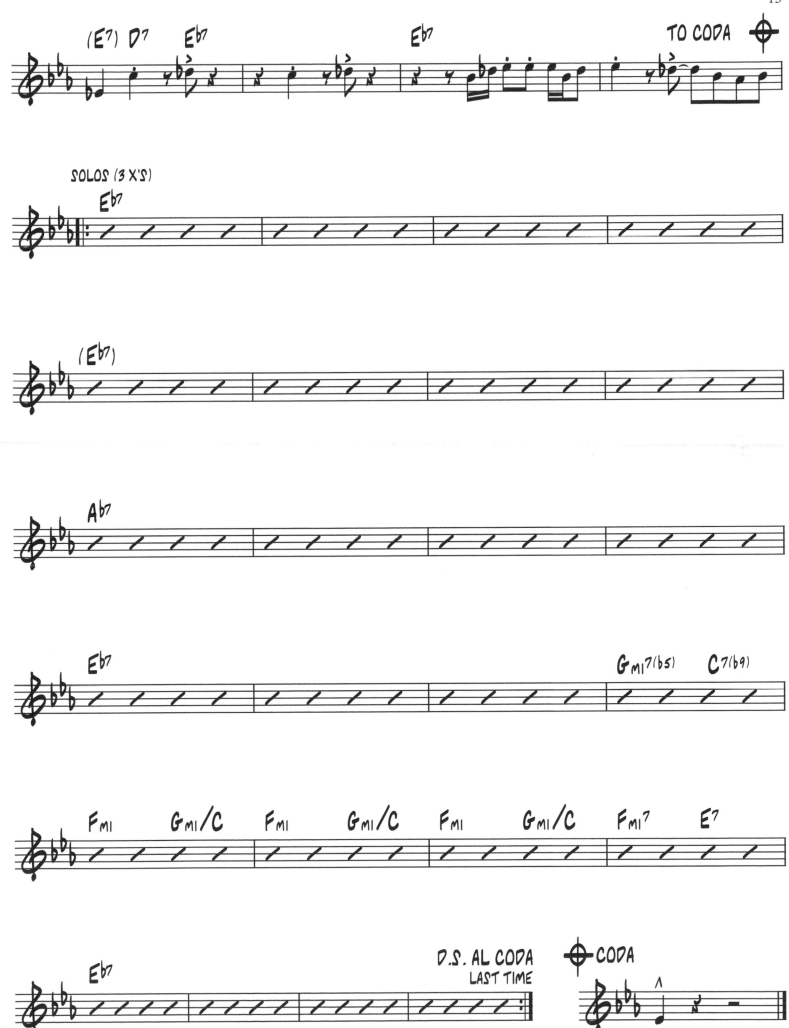

St. Thomas

C Version

BY SONNY ROLLINS

STOLEN MOMENTS

C VERSION

WORDS AND MUSIC BY OLIVER NELSON

WELL YOU NEEDN'T

IT'S OVER NOW

ENGLISH LYRIC BY MIKE FERRO
MUSIC BY THELONIOUS MONK

C VERSION

Bb LEAD SHEETS

BLUE TRAIN

Bb Version

BY JOHN COLTRANE

COMIN' HOME BABY

B♭ Version

SOUL JAZZ

BY BOB DOROUGH AND BEN TUCKER

Footprints

B♭ Version

BY WAYNE SHORTER

IMPRESSIONS

Bb Version

By John Coltrane

Killer Joe

Bᵇ Version

BY BENNY GOLSON

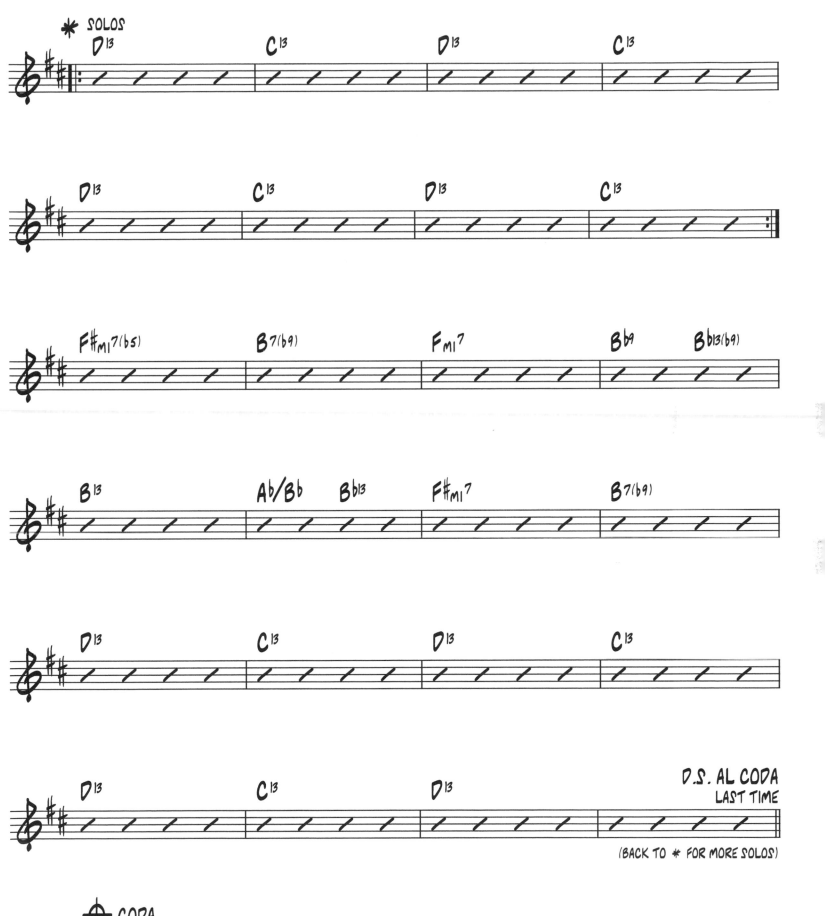

MOANIN'

Bb VERSION

BY BOBBY TIMMONS

Sidewinder

Bᵇ Version

BY LEE MORGAN

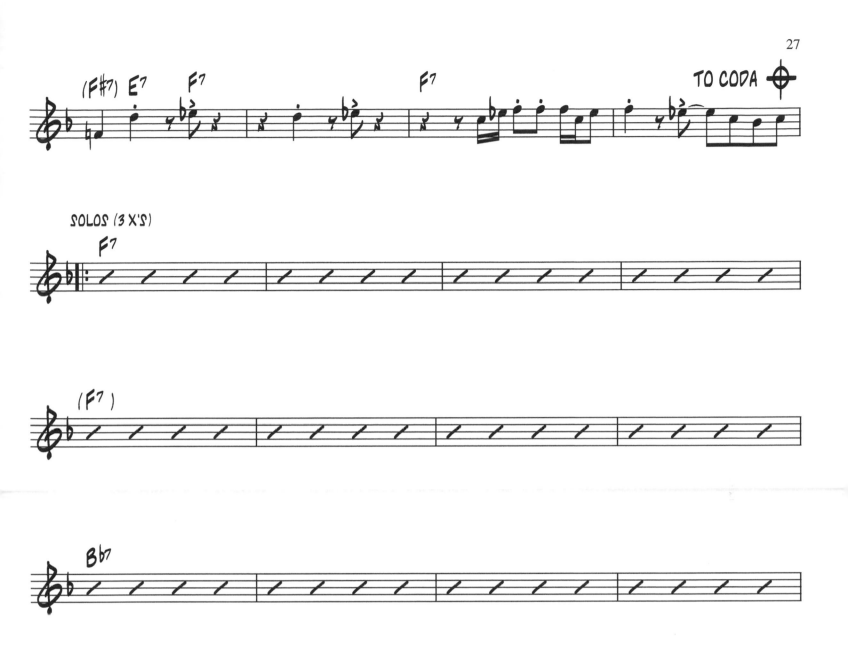

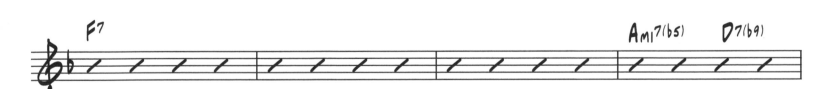

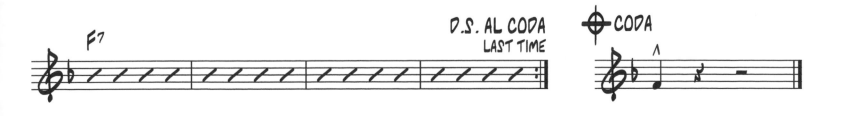

St. Thomas

Bb Version

BY SONNY ROLLINS

STOLEN MOMENTS

Bb Version

WORDS AND MUSIC BY OLIVER NELSON

WELL YOU NEEDN'T

IT'S OVER NOW

ENGLISH LYRIC BY MIKE FERRO
MUSIC BY THELONIOUS MONK

Bb VERSION

MEDIUM SWING

Eb LEAD SHEETS

BLUE TRAIN

Eb Version

BY JOHN COLTRANE

COMIN' HOME BABY

Eb Version

BY BOB DOROUGH AND BEN TUCKER

FOOTPRINTS

Eb VERSION

BY WAYNE SHORTER

IMPRESSIONS

E♭ Version

By John Coltrane

KILLER JOE

Eb VERSION

BY BENNY GOLSON

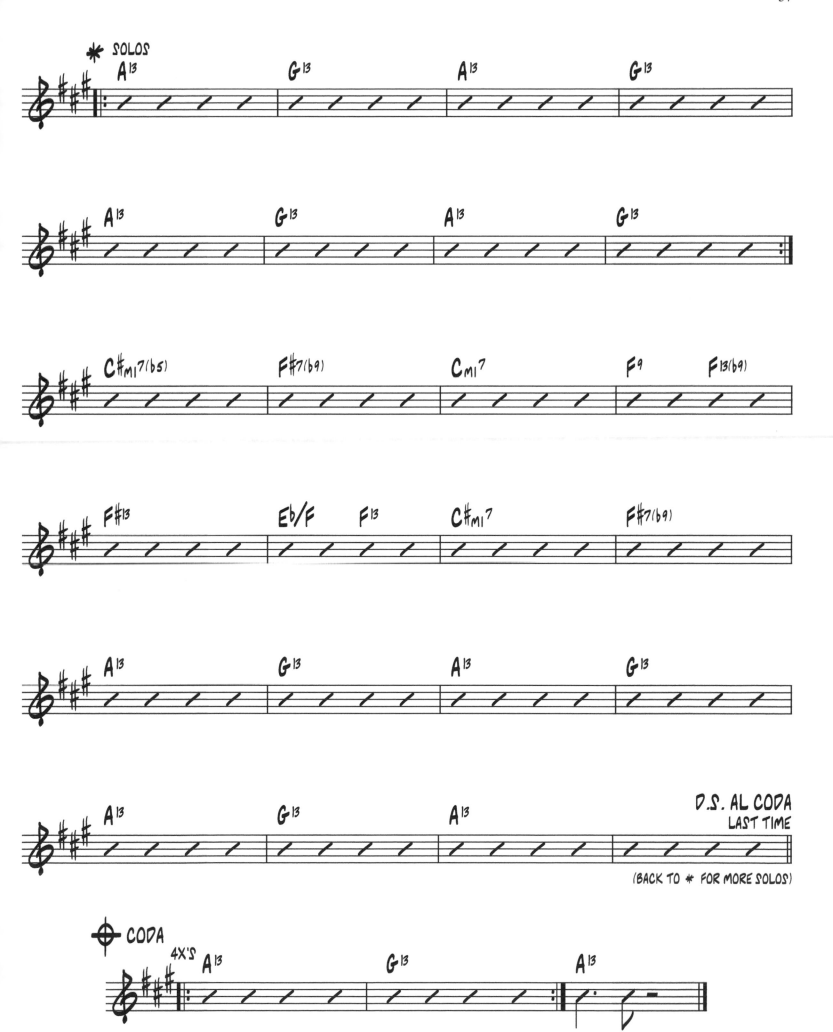

MOANIN'

Eᵇ VERSION

BY BOBBY TIMMONS

Sidewinder

Eᵇ Version

By Lee Morgan

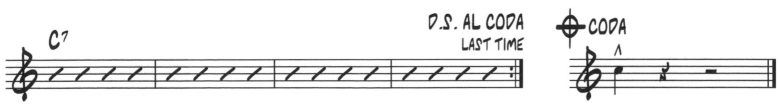

St. Thomas

E♭ Version

BY SONNY ROLLINS

STOLEN MOMENTS

Eb Version

WORDS AND MUSIC BY OLIVER NELSON

WELL YOU NEEDN'T

IT'S OVER NOW

English Lyric by Mike Ferro
Music by Thelonious Monk

Eb Version

𝄢 C LEAD SHEETS

BLUE TRAIN

9: C VERSION

BY JOHN COLTRANE

COMIN' HOME BABY

C Version

BY BOB DOROUGH AND BEN TUCKER

Footprints

C Version

BY WAYNE SHORTER

IMPRESSIONS

BY JOHN COLTRANE

Killer Joe

BY BENNY GOLSON

🎼: C VERSION

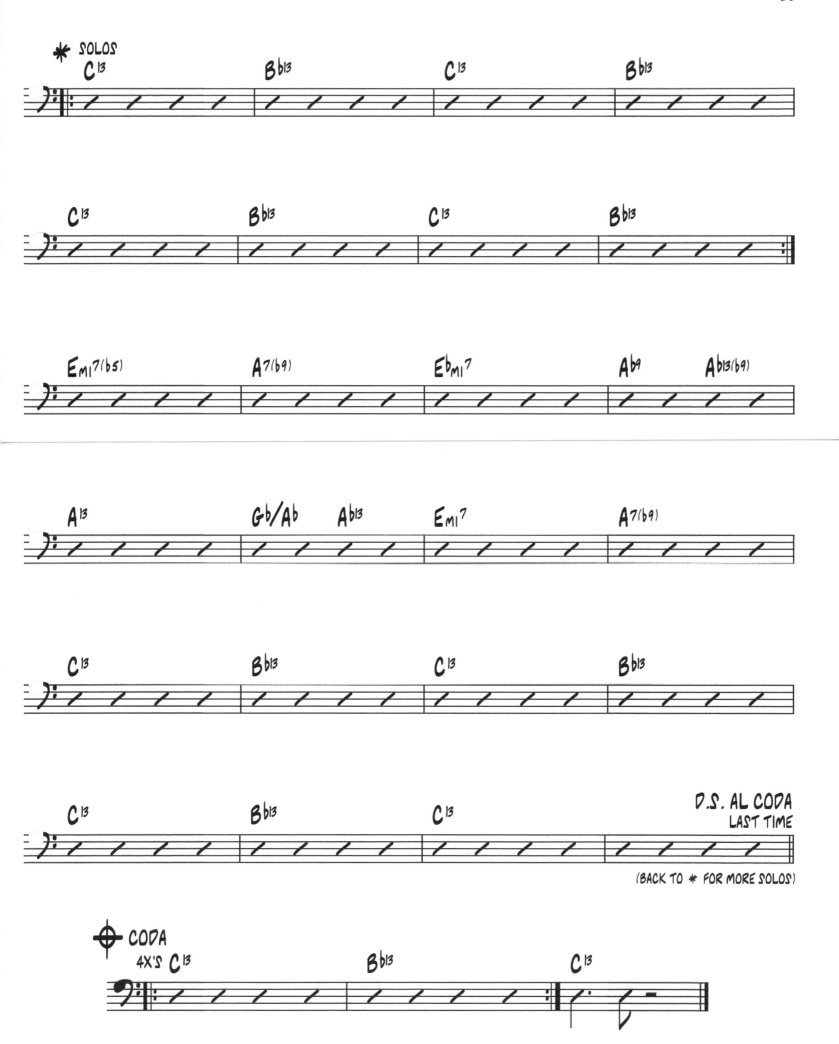

MOANIN'

BY BOBBY TIMMONS

SIDEWINDER

♩: C VERSION

By Lee Morgan

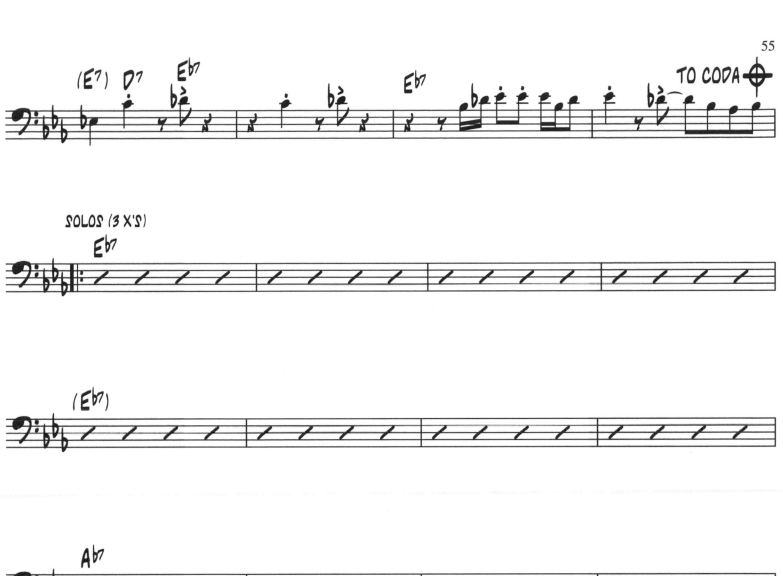

St. Thomas

STOLEN MOMENTS

C Version

WORDS AND MUSIC BY OLIVER NELSON

WELL YOU NEEDN'T

IT'S OVER NOW

ENGLISH LYRIC BY MIKE FERRO
MUSIC BY THELONIOUS MONK

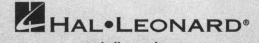

The Best-Selling Jazz Book of All Time Is Now Legal!

The Real Books are the most popular jazz books of all time. Since the 1970s, musicians have trusted these volumes to get them through every gig, night after night. The problem is that the books were illegally produced and distributed, without any regard to copyright law, or royalties paid to the composers who created these musical masterpieces.

Hal Leonard is very proud to present the first legitimate and legal editions of these books ever produced. You won't even notice the difference, other than all the notorious errors being fixed: the covers and typeface look the same, the song lists are nearly identical, and the price for our edition is even cheaper than the originals!

Every conscientious musician will appreciate that these books are now produced accurately and ethically, benefitting the songwriters that we owe for some of the greatest tunes of all time!

VOLUME 1
00240221	C Edition	$49.99
00240224	B♭ Edition	$49.99
00240225	E♭ Edition	$49.99
00240226	Bass Clef Edition	$49.99
00286389	F Edition	$39.99
00240292	C Edition 6 x 9	$39.99
00240339	B♭ Edition 6 x 9	$44.99
00147792	Bass Clef Edition 6 x 9	$39.99
00200984	Online Backing Tracks: Selections	$45.00
00110604	Book/USB Flash Drive Backing Tracks Pack	$85.00
00110599	USB Flash Drive Only	$50.00

VOLUME 2
00240222	C Edition	$49.99
00240227	B♭ Edition	$49.99
00240228	E♭ Edition	$49.99
00240229	Bass Clef Edition	$49.99
00240293	C Edition 6 x 9	$39.99
00125900	B♭ Edition 6 x 9	$39.99
00125900	The Real Book – Mini Edition	$39.99
00204126	Backing Tracks on USB Flash Drive	$55.00
00204131	C Edition – USB Flash Drive Pack	$85.00

VOLUME 3
00240233	C Edition	$49.99
00240284	B♭ Edition	$49.99
00240285	E♭ Edition	$49.99
00240286	Bass Clef Edition	$49.99
00240338	C Edition 6 x 9	$39.99

VOLUME 4
00240296	C Edition	$49.99
00103348	B♭ Edition	$49.99
00103349	E♭ Edition	$49.99
00103350	Bass Clef Edition	$49.99

VOLUME 5
00240349	C Edition	$49.99
00175278	B♭ Edition	$49.99
00175279	E♭ Edition	$49.99

VOLUME 6
00240534	C Edition	$49.99
00223637	E♭ Edition	$49.99

Also available:
00154230	The Real Bebop Book C Edition	$34.99
00295069	The Real Bebop Book E♭ Edition	$34.99
00295068	The Real Bebop Book B♭ Edition	$34.99
00240264	The Real Blues Book	$39.99
00310910	The Real Bluegrass Book	$39.99
00240223	The Real Broadway Book	$39.99
00240440	The Trane Book	$25.00
00125426	The Real Country Book	$45.00
00269721	The Real Miles Davis Book C Edition	$29.99
00269723	The Real Miles Davis Book B♭ Edition	$29.99
00240355	The Real Dixieland Book C Edition	$39.99
00294853	The Real Dixieland Book E♭ Edition	$39.99
00122335	The Real Dixieland Book B♭ Edition	$39.99
00240235	The Duke Ellington Real Book	$29.99
00240268	The Real Jazz Solos Book	$44.99
00240348	The Real Latin Book C Edition	$39.99
00127107	The Real Latin Book B♭ Edition	$39.99
00120809	The Pat Metheny Real Book C Edition	$34.99
00252119	The Pat Metheny Real Book B♭ Edition	$29.99
00240358	The Charlie Parker Real Book C Edition	$25.00
00275997	The Charlie Parker Real Book E♭ Edition	$25.00
00118324	The Real Pop Book C Edition – Vol. 1	$45.00
00295066	The Real Pop Book B♭ Edition – Vol. 1	$39.99
00286451	The Real Pop Book C Edition – Vol. 2	$45.00
00240331	The Bud Powell Real Book	$25.00
00240437	The Real R&B Book C Edition	$45.00
00276590	The Real R&B Book B♭ Edition	$45.00
00240313	The Real Rock Book	$39.99
00240323	The Real Rock Book – Vol. 2	$39.99
00240359	The Real Tab Book	$39.99
00240317	The Real Worship Book	$35.00

THE REAL CHRISTMAS BOOK
00240306	C Edition	$39.99
00240345	B♭ Edition	$35.00
00240346	E♭ Edition	$35.00
00240347	Bass Clef Edition	$35.00

THE REAL VOCAL BOOK
00240230	Volume 1 High Voice	$40.00
00240307	Volume 1 Low Voice	$40.00
00240231	Volume 2 High Voice	$39.99
00240308	Volume 2 Low Voice	$39.99
00240391	Volume 3 High Voice	$39.99
00240392	Volume 3 Low Voice	$39.99
00118318	Volume 4 High Voice	$39.99
00118319	Volume 4 Low Voice	$39.99

Complete song lists online at www.halleonard.com

0223
318